WARWICK CASTLE
THE LIVING HISTORY

THE ORIGINS OF WARWICK CASTLE CAN BE TRACED BACK TO THE SAXON FORTIFICATION WHICH ETHELFLEDA, DAUGHTER OF ALFRED THE GREAT, USED TO DEFEND AGAINST THE INVADING DANES. THE FIRST CASTLE HOWEVER, TO APPEAR ON THE SITE WAS A WOODEN MOTTE AND BAILEY CONSTRUCTED IN 1068 AT THE COMMAND OF WILLIAM THE CONQUEROR. THROUGHOUT THE MIDDLE AGES, UNDER SUCCESSIVE EARLS OF WARWICK, THE CASTLE WAS GRADUALLY REBUILT IN STONE. BY THE 14TH CENTURY, IT WAS A TOWERING MEDIAEVAL FORTRESS AND THE STRONGHOLD OF THE MIGHTY BEAUCHAMP FAMILY. LATER AS THE CASTLE DECLINED IN MILITARY IMPORTANCE, THE MAIN LIVING QUARTERS WERE CONVERTED INTO A RESIDENCE OF RICH AND SUMPTUOUS STYLE THAT REFLECTED THE WEALTH AND STATUS OF ITS OWNERS. ATTACKED IN 1264, BESIEGED IN 1642 AND DAMAGED BY FIRE IN 1871, THE CASTLE HAS NEVERTHELESS GLORIOUSLY SURVIVED THE EVER-CHANGING FORTUNES OF HISTORY, AND STANDS TODAY AS THE MOST IMPRESSIVE OF ENGLAND'S ANCIENT FORTRESSES. THE CASTLE WAS HOME TO THE EARLS OF WARWICK UNTIL 1978, WHEN IT WAS BOUGHT BY THE TUSSAUDS GROUP. SINCE THEN EXTENSIVE RESTORATION WORK HAS BEEN CARRIED OUT AND SUBSTANTIAL AREAS OF THE CASTLE, WHICH WERE PREVIOUSLY CLOSED TO THE PUBLIC, HAVE BEEN OPENED. WE HOPE YOUR VISIT WILL BE PLEASURABLE AND REWARDING.

East aspect of Warwick Castle at dawn.

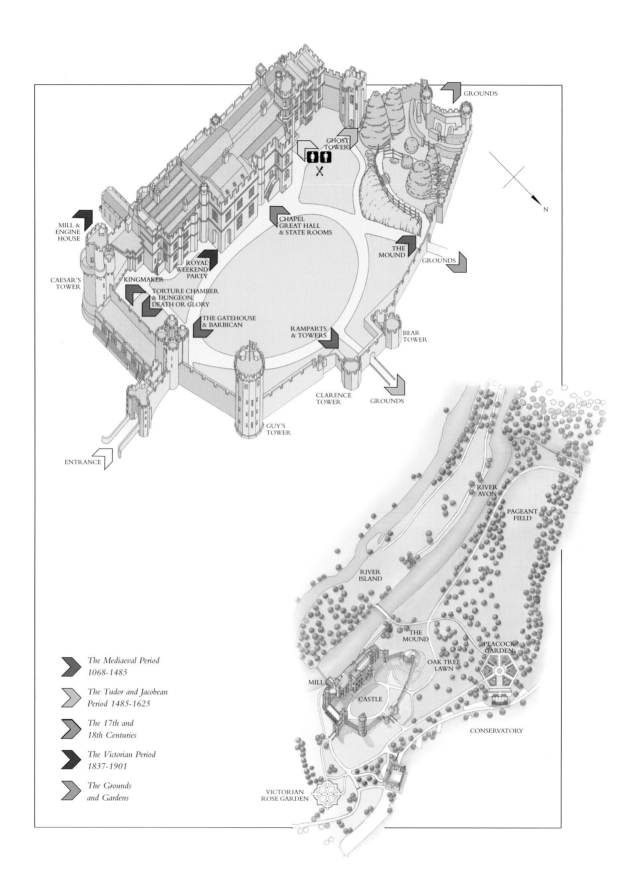

GROUNDS

GHOST
TOWER

CHAPEL
GREAT HALL
& STATE ROOMS

THE
MOUND

GROUNDS

N

MILL &
ENGINE
HOUSE

CAESAR'S
TOWER

KINGMAKER

ROYAL
WEEKEND
PARTY

TORTURE CHAMBER
& DUNGEON,
DEATH OR GLORY

THE GATEHOUSE
& BARBICAN

RAMPARTS
& TOWERS

BEAR
TOWER

CLARENCE
TOWER

GROUNDS

GUY'S
TOWER

ENTRANCE

RIVER
AVON

PAGEANT
FIELD

RIVER
ISLAND

THE
MOUND

PEACOCK
GARDEN

OAK TREE
LAWN

MILL

CASTLE

CONSERVATORY

VICTORIAN
ROSE GARDEN

The Mediaeval Period
1068-1485

The Tudor and Jacobean
Period 1485-1625

The 17th and
18th Centuries

The Victorian Period
1837-1901

The Grounds
and Gardens

THE HISTORY OF WARWICK CASTLE   4–13

DEATH OR GLORY, THE ARMOURY   14–15

KINGMAKER   16–21

THE TOWERS & RAMPARTS   22–24

THE DUNGEON   25

THE GHOST TOWER   26–27

THE STATE ROOMS

The Chapel   28–29

The State Dining Room   30–31

The Great Hall   32–34

The Red Drawing Room   35

The Cedar Drawing Room   36

The Green Drawing Room   37

The Queen Anne Bedroom   38

The Blue Boudoir   39

A ROYAL WEEKEND PARTY, 1898

The Library   40

The Music Room   41

The Smoking Room   41

The Ladies' Boudoir   42

Daisy's Bedroom   43

The Carnation Bedroom   43

The Dowager's Bedroom   44

The Earl's Dressing Room   44

The Kenilworth Bedroom   45

The Chinese Bedroom   45

MILL & ENGINE HOUSE   46

THE GROUNDS   47–51

WARWICK CASTLE TODAY   52

 AUDIO TOURS

Throughout the castle there are a series of audio tour signs, each with its own number. The number on the sign relates to the corresponding number on the audio tour. Matching the two, you will be able to hear the commentary on the part of the castle in which you see the sign.

To help find your way around, you will see a series of signs at relevant points around the castle and the grounds. These signs are colour-coded to match the different periods in the castle's history.

The page numbers in the guidebook are each contained in a coloured panel. As with the castle signs, the colour of the panel is coded according to the historical period that particular section of the guidebook is describing.

THE HISTORY OF WARWICK CASTLE

THERE HAS BEEN A FORTIFICATION OF SOME DESCRIPTION OVERLOOKING THIS PART OF THE
RIVER AVON FROM AS FAR BACK AS AD914.

THE EARLS OF WARWICK

de Newburgh	1088 – 1119	HENRY DE NEWBURGH
	1119 – 1153	ROGER DE NEWBURGH
	1153 – 1184	WILLIAM DE NEWBURGH
	1184 – 1203	WALERAN DE NEWBURGH
	1203 – 1229	HENRY DE NEWBURGH
	1229 – 1242	THOMAS DE NEWBURGH
du Plessis	1242 – 1263	JOHN DU PLESSIS
	1263 – 1268	WILLIAM MAUDUIT
	1268 – 1298	WILLIAM DE BEAUCHAMP
	1298 – 1315	GUY DE BEAUCHAMP
	1329 – 1369	THOMAS DE BEAUCHAMP
	1369 – 1401	THOMAS DE BEAUCHAMP
	1401 – 1439	RICHARD BEAUCHAMP
Mauduit	1439 – 1446	HENRY BEAUCHAMP *also first and only Duke, 1445-1446*
	1446 – 1449	ANNE BEAUCHAMP
	1449 – 1471	RICHARD NEVILLE *The Kingmaker*
de Beauchamp	1472 – 1478	GEORGE PLANTAGENET *Duke of Clarence*
	1478 – 1499	EDWARD PLANTAGENET
	1499 – 1547	CROWN PROPERTY *1499-1509, Henry VII* *1509-1547, Henry VIII*
Neville	1547 – 1553	JOHN DUDLEY I
	1553 – 1554	JOHN DUDLEY II
	1561 – 1590	AMBROSE DUDLEY
	1590 – 1604	CROWN PROPERTY *1590-1603, Elizabeth I* *1603-1604, James I*
Plantagenet	1604 – 1628	SIR FULKE GREVILLE *owned the castle as Baron Brooke while the Earldom was held by the Rich family. The Greville's were granted the Earldom in 1759*
	1618 – 1619	ROBERT RICH I
	1619 – 1658	ROBERT RICH II
	1621 – 1628	SIR FULKE GREVILLE
	1658 – 1659	ROBERT RICH III
	1659 – 1673	CHARLES RICH
Dudley	1673 – 1675	ROBERT RICH IV
	1675 – 1701	EDWARD RICH I
	1701 – 1721	EDWARD HENRY RICH
	1721 – 1759	EDWARD RICH II
Rich	1759 – 1773	FRANCIS GREVILLE
	1773 – 1816	GEORGE GREVILLE
	1816 – 1853	HENRY RICHARD GREVILLE
	1853 – 1893	GEORGE GUY GREVILLE
	1893 – 1924	FRANCIS RICHARD GREVILLE
	1924 – 1928	LEOPOLD GUY GREVILLE
	1928 – 1984	CHARLES GUY GREVILLE
	1984 – 1996	DAVID GREVILLE
Greville	1996 –	GUY GREVILLE

All the above dates refer to the length of time the person concerned held either the title of Earl of Warwick or that of Baron Brooke.

The earliest military strategist to make use of the area's defensive features was Ethelfleda, daughter of Alfred the Great.

With Danish invaders threatening Mercia, the central Anglo-Saxon kingdom, Ethelfleda ordered the building in AD914 of a 'burh' or an earthen rampart to protect the small hill top settlement of Warwick.

It was, in fact, another invader who was responsible for the first true castle built on the present site. William the Conqueror, wanting to consolidate the Norman Conquest in the midlands and north of England, established a motte and bailey fort here in 1068 as a means of holding the area and securing his lines of supply.

William appointed one of his followers, Henry de Beaumont (c.1088-1119), as Castellan or Constable. The castle would then have consisted of a large earth mound with a timber stockade around both the top and base. It was not until later in the 12th century that stone structures started to replace these wooden ones.

At some point during his stewardship, de Beaumont underwent a change of name and became known, at least locally, as de Newburgh. Five of his descendants duly followed in their forefather's footsteps as Earls of Warwick. The last of these, Thomas, died in 1242 without an heir and the castle and estates passed to his sister Margaret.

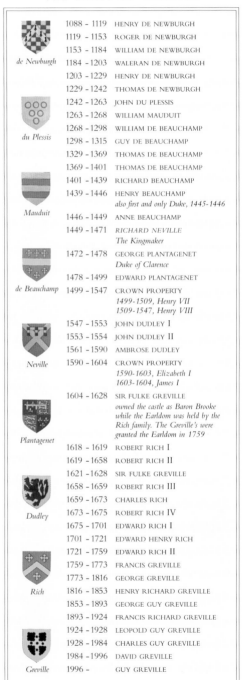

THE CASTLE c.1070

The first castle at Warwick would have consisted of a man-made motte, or mound, built on the cliff overlooking the river. Crowning the mound was a wooden stockade, inside which probably stood a commanding square timber tower. Ranged in front of the motte and divided from it by a ditch was the bailey. Wooden buildings would have hugged the inside of the palissade. On the river side were a thatched hall, a plain chapel, a kitchen, bake house and brewhouse, while opposite would probably have been housing for the soldiery and stabling for the horses, along with the blacksmith's and an armour shop.

	1066	1068	1084	1088
AT WARWICK CASTLE		*William I orders castle to be built*		*1st Earl of Warwick created by William I*

| THE WORLD | *Battle of Hastings* | | *Rome sacked by the Norman army* | |

By 1220, the castle had undergone a major transformation. In almost all of its architecture, stone had replaced wood as the principal building material. Vanished was the Norman stockade: instead what is known as the 'shell keep', a circular tower with thick, crenellated walls and fighting platforms for its soldiers, topped the mound. The bailey also boasted a new defensive system. A 7.6m stone curtain wall surrounded it, reinforced on the north by two towers and an imposing gatehouse and drawbridge and by additional towers on the east and west sides. The chapel and hall, from where the earl administered the estate, were now also of stone.

Margaret's marriage to John du Plessis (1242-63) was childless and, as a consequence, in 1263 the title changed hands once more, the mantle this time falling to her cousin William Mauduit.

Mauduit suffered the misfortune of becoming Earl during the Barons' War, a violent trial of strength between Henry III and a group of dissident nobles resentful of Henry's court policies.

William sided with the king. In the event this proved not an altogether wise move since Kenilworth Castle, the stronghold of Simon de Montfort, Earl of Leicester and leader of the rebellious barons, lay just 8 kilometres away.

Despite the alarming proximity of his enemy, Mauduit did little to prepare for the defence of Warwick Castle. It was no surprise therefore, except perhaps to William himself, when John Giffard, Governor of Kenilworth, attacked in 1264, breached the castle walls, captured Mauduit and his wife and held them to ransom.

N

1153	1161	1215	1260
Garrison tricked into handing castle to Henry of Anjou's men			*Stone starts to replace wood*
	Chinese use explosives in warfare	*King John signs Magna Carta*	*Chartres Cathedral completed*

Constable's room in the 14th century Gatehouse.

On his death in 1268, Mauduit was succeeded by his nephew William de Beauchamp. So began a dynasty that was to last 148 years and bring Warwick Castle to the height of its fortunes.

William de Beauchamp (1268-98) made his name as a military commander serving under Edward I.

Reflecting the growing importance of the de Beauchamps, his son Guy (1298-1315) was one of a group of earls known as the Ordainers.

With their own interests firmly at heart, they aimed to impose, through a list of 'ordinances' or constitutional demands, some form of control over the way the king, Edward II, both raised his revenue and governed the kingdom.

For some Ordainers, complaints about royal power (especially royal spending power) centred on the role at court of Piers Gaveston, a Gascon knight and the king's lover.

At a time of heightened political tension in 1312, Gaveston, promised that his life would be safe, surrendered to the Ordainer earls. However, Guy de Beauchamp seized the prisoner and brought him to Warwick Castle. After a perfunctory trial, which may have been held in the Great Hall, Gaveston was sentenced to death and beheaded on Blacklow Hill, just outside Warwick.

Although Guy died three years later in 1315, his very young son did not succeed to the title until 1329 because of his minority. Thomas de Beauchamp (1329-69) came of age on the verge of the outbreak of the Hundred Years War with France.

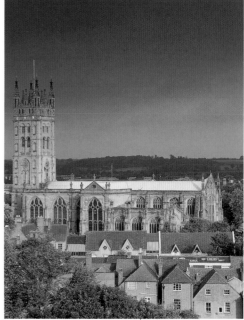

The Collegiate Church of St Mary, Warwick.

	1264		1268		1312		1314
AT WARWICK CASTLE	*Castle successfully attacked by Simon de Montfort*		*The de Beauchamps succeed as Earls of Warwick*		*Piers Gaveston held at Warwick Castle prior to his execution*		

THE WORLD					*Scots defeat English at Bannockburn*

In 1337 Edward III restated the claim of the Plantagenets to the French throne and, in 1338, the long conflict began.

Thomas emerged as one of the king's favoured commanders. He fought at Crecy (1346) and Poitiers (1356) and was among the first men to be made a Knight of the Garter. Such was his position in the ranks of the English army that he became military adviser to Edward III's son, the Black Prince.

It was Thomas, too, who started the massive 14th century reconstruction of Warwick Castle.

The fate of his son, Thomas the younger (1370-97, 1399-1401), was bound up with the domestic feuds and political purges which marked the reign of Richard II. In another contest of wills between elements of the nobility and the crown, Thomas and four other lords forced Richard, at the 'Merciless Parliament' of 1388, to dismiss or execute some of his court favourites.

In 1397, Richard had his revenge. Sensing that political circumstances were on his side, he brought the lords of 1388 to trial. Warwick confessed to treachery. He was exiled to the Isle of Man and his lands and title were forfeited. It was only when Richard was usurped by Henry Bolingbroke (Henry IV) in 1399 that Thomas could return to reclaim his inheritance.

The next in line, Thomas' son Richard (1401-39), became perhaps the most prominent Beauchamp of all. Like his grandfather before him, Richard's reputation was forged during an intense phase of the Hundred Years War.

Henry V had faith enough in his abilities to make him tutor to his young son, the future Henry VI.

Richard Beauchamp, 1401-1439.

Far left:
The Beauchamp Chapel, Church of St Mary, Warwick, showing the tombs of Richard Beauchamp and Ambrose Dudley (foreground).

1339	1356	c.1395	1431
	French soldiers and nobles reputedly held as prisoners	*Guy's Tower completed*	*Earl of Warwick supervises trial of Joan of Arc*
Kremlin built			

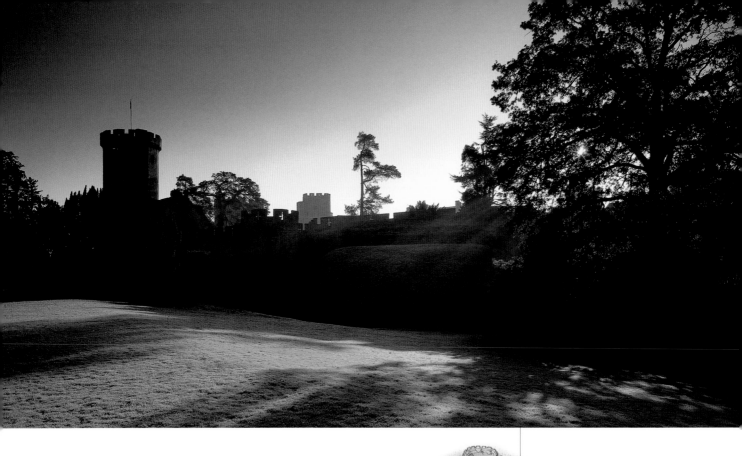

When, in 1431, the English bought the captive Joan of Arc for a ransom fee, it fell to Richard Beauchamp, as Captain of Calais, to superintend her trial for supposed heresy and her subsequent execution by burning in the market place at Rouen in northern France.

War proved profitable for Richard. It certainly made him enough money to continue with the expensive rebuilding programme at the castle.

Richard's son, Henry (1439-46), had grown up as a companion to the boy King Henry VI. In 1445, the king made his childhood friend the first Duke of Warwick. But he was also the last, the title dying with him in the very next year.

Henry was survived only by a baby daughter and when she died at the age of five the earldom and lands passed to Henry's sister, Anne Beauchamp. In the late 1440s Anne married Richard Neville and the de Beauchamp dynasty came to an end.

No Earl of Warwick held sway in the kingdom to quite the extent that Neville did, albeit briefly. Throughout the course of the Wars of the Roses, Warwick, in helping to depose both Henry VI and Edward IV, won himself the title of Kingmaker.

But the ambition that lifted him to such heights led also to his downfall. On Neville's defeat and death at the battle of Barnet in 1471, the castle and the estates were awarded by Edward IV to his own brother, George, Duke of Clarence.

Clarence had a history of disloyalty (at one time he had been Neville's ally in the Wars of the Roses) and, despite his defection to Edward IV, he had never really taken his eyes off the throne. Suspected of intriguing against Edward, he was imprisoned and killed in 1478.

THE CASTLE c.1450

Throughout the 14th and 15th centuries, a massive rebuilding programme transformed Warwick Castle yet again. Now rising into the sky were the two colossal towers that still dominate the east of the castle: imposing itself on the river was Caesar's Tower with its stepped base; while to the right was twelve-sided Guy's Tower. Between them lay the gatehouse to which had been added another protective structure called a barbican, extending out into the ditch and housing the drawbridge. A potential weak point in the castle's defences, the south-western flank of the wall facing the river, was bolstered by the building of the Watergate Tower. Two-storied lean-to barracks now clustered either side of Guy's Tower, and extra rooms were added to the Chapel and Great Hall.

1469

AT WARWICK CASTLE

Edward IV imprisoned at the castle

1471

Richard Neville, Kingmaker, dies at Battle of Barnet

1492

8

THE WORLD

Columbus reaches New World

One last knot was to tie Warwick Castle to the Wars of the Roses. After the execution of Clarence, his brother, Richard of Gloucester (future King Richard III), took possession of the castle. His wife Anne was Neville's younger daughter.

The title Earl of Warwick was retained by Clarence's son, Edward (1478-99), though it brought him little good. As the last Plantagenet (and therefore a possible rival to the Tudor king, Henry VII), he was kept in the Tower of London. There he lingered from 1485 until 1499 when he was executed for allegedly conspiring with the second of the two pretenders to the throne, Perkin Warbeck.

There was no natural successor to Edward and the castle stayed as property of the crown. Under Henry VIII work was carried out to reinforce the walls on the river front.

In 1547, however, a young Edward VI granted the rightful title to John Dudley, a member of the Protectorate which had been set up to help the 9-year old king rule in the years immediately after the death of Henry VIII.

From 1550, the new Earl of Warwick exercised immense influence in the running of the country. But Edward's ill-health made his position less than totally secure and the king's early death in 1553 left Dudley facing what he had long feared: the prospect of Edward's sister, Mary, ascending the throne and his own fall from power.

His response, in a move which had Edward's blessing before he died, was to place his daughter-in-law, Lady Jane Grey, on the throne. The coup, its support melting away, lasted barely two weeks. It ended with Mary Tudor reclaiming her right to rule and with Dudley, his son Guilford and Lady Jane Grey executed for treason.

Under Elizabeth I, who succeeded Mary, the Dudley family found itself back in favour. Elizabeth not only created Ambrose Dudley, Guilford's brother, Earl of Warwick (1561-90), she also granted him the castle. Ambrose died in 1590 without an heir and the estate reverted back to the Crown.

In 1604, James I presented the by now dilapidated castle to Sir Fulke Greville. (The title Earl of Warwick, however, was conferred on Lord Rich in 1618 and it remained in his family until 1759).

Caesar's Tower viewed from the River Avon.

THE CASTLE c.1540
In the 1480s the castle was held by the Duke of Gloucester, later Richard III, and it was he who ordered the construction of an additional tower on the north wall. This huge square building was to have been a self-sufficient defensive bastion, an insurance against any mutinous attack by the castle's own garrison. Richard's death in 1485 meant that only two corner towers, known as the Bear and Clarence Towers, were built and at a much lower height than was planned. During the reign of Henry VIII, the kitchen was rebuilt. The 16th century also saw the appearance of the Spy Tower and the lower sections of the domestic buildings to the left of the Great Hall. About this time, too, the natural rock of the cliff face was reinforced to help distribute the weight of the walls above and stop the erosion of the bedrock below.

c.1504

Leonardo da Vinci paints Mona Lisa

1572
Elizabeth I visits Warwick Castle

1604
James I grants castle to Sir Fulke Greville

9

The earliest known painting of Warwick Castle (c.1695).

Greville, who had already served Elizabeth in office, was James I's Chancellor of the Exchequer for a number of years. When he left the post, in 1621, Greville (coming from an age when it was possible to be a poet, a courtier and a public servant) was elevated to the peerage as Baron Brooke.

Following his murder at the hands of his discontented manservant, the estate went to his adopted heir, Robert Greville, 2nd Lord Brooke.

At the outset of the Civil War, he was appointed Commander of Parliamentary forces in Staffordshire and Warwickshire. In August 1642, the castle, under Sir Edward Peyto, saw off a feeble siege by royalist troops.

After Robert Greville's death, in action at Lichfield, the castle passed to each of his three sons over the next few years. It went first to his eldest, Francis (1643-58), and then to a younger son, Robert (1658-77).

Not apparently sharing his father's radical, idealistic outlook, Robert played a part in the restoration of the monarchy in 1660.

Like Francis, he died without any children and it was the turn of the third brother to inherit. Fulke Greville, 5th Lord Brooke (1677-1710), was elected to Parliament and helped with the repair of the town of Warwick after a disastrous fire in 1694.

The 8th Lord Brooke, Francis Greville, married Elizabeth, the sister of Sir William Hamilton. This was the same William Hamilton whose wife Emma enjoyed a tempestuous and public affair with Lord Nelson.

THE CASTLE c.1700
When the castle was besieged by Royalists in the English Civil War, a number of defensive measures were taken. Cannon were positioned on the mound, and gun emplacements were established in the guard room at the top of Guy's Tower. The east side of the shell keep, the semi-circled stone walling on top of the mound, still remained. By 1670, the building now housing Death or Glory, initially used as a laundry, washhouse and brewhouse, had been built against the east wall between Caesar's Tower and the gatehouse.

	1633	1642	c.1665	1695	1707	1750	1763
AT WARWICK CASTLE		Siege of the castle by Royalist troops		King William III visits the castle		'Capability' Brown engaged to lay out grounds	State Dining Room commissioned
THE WORLD	St Peter's in Rome completed		Isaac Newton discovers law of gravity		Union of England and Scotland		

View of Warwick Castle
by the Buck Brothers.
Dated 1729.

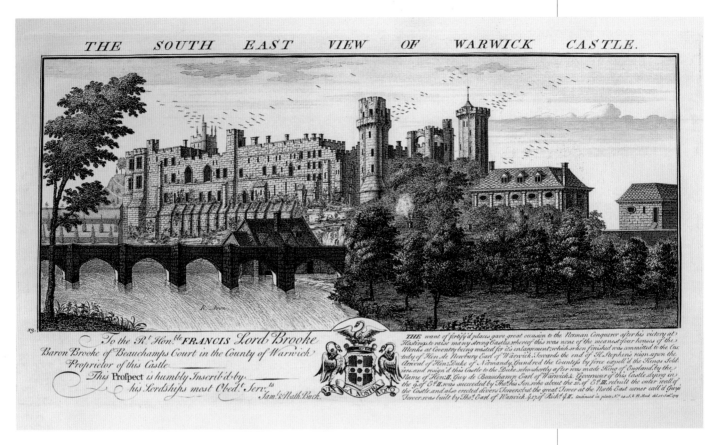

THE SOUTH EAST VIEW OF WARWICK CASTLE.

To the R.t Hon.ble FRANCIS Lord Brooke
Baron Brooke of Beauchamps Court in the County of Warwick
Proprietor of this Castle
This Prospect is humbly Inscrib'd by
his Lordships most Obed.t Serv.ts
Jam.s & Nath. Buck.

When the Rich family died out in 1759, Francis successfully petitioned for
the title Earl of Warwick, so reuniting the earldom and the castle once more. In
the 1750s he commissioned Lancelot 'Capability' Brown to landscape the gardens.

His son George Greville (1773-1816) showed an equal zeal for improving the
look and style of the castle. He put the finishing touches to the State Rooms and
bought many of the paintings and pieces of furniture now on display.
Unfortunately, his enthusiasm ran somewhat ahead of his
bank account. By 1804 he was forced to sell off outlying
estates in order to keep himself solvent.

THE CASTLE c.1800

The refurbishment of the living quarters
began in the 17th century and continued
in resplendent lavish style throughout the
18th century. Along with several other
alterations, a magnificent new dining
room was added to the State Rooms in
1763. Many elegant changes also took
place in the grounds. The mound was
given an attractive make-over with two
new towers and a parapet walk. The
gardens were formally laid out to plans by
'Capability' Brown, who also redesigned
the courtyard. A gateway was added
between the Bear and Clarence Towers,
and the castle grounds expanded to
the north and east. In 1796, the entrance
lodge and main driveway were
constructed. By 1800, as seen from the
outside, the castle was as it is today,
although a fire in 1871 meant that many
of the private apartments had to be
extensively refurbished.

1770	1786	1789	1815	1858	1861	1871	1894
Warwick vase found near Tivoli, Italy	Conservatory built			Queen Victoria lunches at the castle		Fire damages the Great Hall	Engine House first generates electricity to the castle
		George Washington becomes 1st US President	Napoleon defeated at Waterloo		Outbreak of American Civil War		

Finances had become less of a problem by the time Francis Richard Greville (1893-1924) and his wife Frances (Daisy) were holding their high society parties of the 1890s.

Their son Leopold, known as Guy (1924-28), who married Elfrida Marjorie Eden, older sister of the future Prime Minister Anthony Eden, was a Reuter's correspondent in the Russo-Japanese War of 1905 and later a Brigadier General in the Canadian army during World War I.

The 7th Greville Earl, Charles Guy, (1928-84), using the stage name of Michael Brooke, tried his hand at breaking into Hollywood films. His career peaked with a supporting role in Dawn Patrol (1938) starring Errol Flynn and David Niven. He also created a cinema screen on the roof of the castle which is still there today.

In November 1978, his son David sold Warwick Castle to The Tussauds Group.

Above: Queen Victoria (reigned 1837 – 1901) lunched at Warwick Castle in 1858.
Left: The 5th Earl, Francis Richard Greville 1893-1924.

	1914	1923	1938	1939	1961	1978	1979
AT WARWICK CASTLE		*Countess of Warwick Labour candidate for Parliament*	*Earl of Warwick appears in Hollywood film*			*Earl of Warwick's son, David, sells castle to The Tussauds Group*	
THE WORLD	*World War I starts*			*World War II declared*	*1st man in space*		*Margaret Thatcher is Europe's first woman leader*

Since then The Tussauds Group have carried out extensive restoration work and opened up substantial areas of the castle previously closed to the public. In 1982 the Royal Weekend Party was opened which used the expertise of the Tussauds Studios, introducing wax portraits into the castle.

The Victorian Rose Garden was opened by HRH The Princess of Wales in 1986 having been restored back to its original design.

The largest investment has been the multi-million pound Kingmaker attraction, in the mediaeval undercroft which was opened in 1994. HM The Queen and HRH The Duke of Edinburgh were given a tour of Kingmaker during their visit to the castle in November 1996. On this visit Her Majesty also unveiled a commemorative sword.

To mark the millennium, the Armoury was refurbished and the 'Death or Glory' attraction opened in February 2000, telling the stories of battles over the centuries.

In 2002 the Mill & Engine House opened for the first time to the public following significant investment from The Tussauds Group.

Below: Mr Bissell, Mill Manager at Warwick Castle circa 1900.

Below: Unveiled by HM The Queen, this commemorative sword is a replica of a 16th century two-handed broadsword. It measures 5 feet in length and weighs 6.5lbs.

Left: Since The Tussauds Group acquired the castle in 1978, a sum approaching £20 million has been spent on repairs, restoration and refurbishment around the castle and grounds.
From November 1996 to June 1997 structural and masonry restoration work took place on Guy's Tower roof and north wall which cost over £190,000.

1986	1989	1994	1996	2000	2002
HRH the Princess of Wales opens the Victorian Rose Garden		Kingmaker attraction opens in the Undercroft	HM The Queen and HRH The Duke of Edinburgh visit the castle	Warwick Castle enters the new Millennium	Mill & Engine House opens to public for first time
	Berlin Wall falls				HM The Queen's Golden Jubilee

DEATH OR GLORY, THE ARMOURY

THE ARMOURY WAS ADDED TO THE SOUTH-EAST WALL OF THE CASTLE IN 1669. IT WAS USED FIRST AS A BREW-HOUSE AND WASH-HOUSE, AND THEN AS A LIBRARY, BEFORE IT WAS CONVERTED TO ITS EVENTUAL PURPOSE.

The room is divided into three broad historical periods. The first of these, spanning the period from 1000 to 1500, traces the way body armour developed in response to the weapons that were used against it. In the earlier part of this period, soldiers would have worn knee-length coats of chain mail, made by working metal rings into interlocking strands. A typical coat might have weighed between 9 and 13 kilograms and would have allowed the wearer a reasonable degree of mobility.

By the end of the 13th century, however, the increasing firepower of the crossbow and, more especially, of the longbow meant that knights required greater protection than that afforded by mail. The answer was plate armour which, although heavier and more cumbersome, could better withstand the impact of high velocity bolts and arrows. Despite the introduction of tempered plate, the longbow nevertheless still represented a fearsome battlefield weapon. A highly skilled archer could fire up to fifteen arrows a minute and with enough lethal force to penetrate armour even at some distance. Pieces on show include a 14th century broadsword named after Guy of Warwick and some rare German 'Maximilian' half-armour c.1510.

The second section is concerned principally with the 17th century. At the outbreak of the English Civil War in 1642, Robert Greville, who had inherited Warwick Castle from his father's cousin, Fulke Greville, declared himself for Parliament and accepted the post of Commander-in-Chief to the Parliamentary forces in Staffordshire and Warwickshire. In prompt retaliation, Royalists laid siege to the castle which at the time was defended only by a small garrison of soldiers commanded, in the absence of Robert Greville, by Sir Edward Peyto. The besieging forces, however, proved less than effective in their efforts to take the castle, and two weeks after their appearance the Royalists melted away, leaving the ramparts unstormed.

This black iron hat, dating from the mid-17th century, is something of a military rarity. Charles I reportedly wore just such a hat, covered in velvet, at the battle of Naseby in 1645.

Armour worn by Robert Greville, 2nd Lord Brooke.

In the year AD926, as legend has it, the inhabitants of the village of Dunsmow Heath found themselves living in fear of a huge and terrifying beast. The monster in question was a gigantic cow. Athelstan, the king at the time, ordered Guy of Warwick to slay the menace. Guy duly dispatched the cow, or dun cow, and was knighted for his bravery, which helps explain why so many local pubs are called the Dun Cow. Legend has it that this colossal blackened sword, named after Guy of Warwick, is the one used to fell the bovine adversary. It is, in fact, a rare example of a mediaeval two-handed sword, measuring 1.6m and weighing 6.8 kilograms.

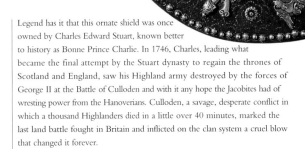

Legend has it that this ornate shield was once owned by Charles Edward Stuart, known better to history as Bonne Prince Charlie. In 1746, Charles, leading what became the final attempt by the Stuart dynasty to regain the thrones of Scotland and England, saw his Highland army destroyed by the forces of George II at the Battle of Culloden and with it any hope the Jacobites had of wresting power from the Hanoverians. Culloden, a savage, desperate conflict in which a thousand Highlanders died in a little over 40 minutes, marked the last land battle fought in Britain and inflicted on the clan system a cruel blow that changed it forever.

Left: Standing in this tent is a British soldier's uniform of the Napoleonic wars. After years of campaigning, Napoleon's ambitions for control of Europe finally came to an end in 1815 at Waterloo, where his French forces were defeated by the armies of the British, under Wellington, the Dutch and the Prussians. One of the most destructive battles (at one point in the day over 45,000 lay dead or wounded in an area of just 4 square kilometres), Waterloo was to shape European history for a hundred years.

Robert Greville himself fought at the battle of Edgehill in 1642 and later, in 1643, at the siege of Lichfield where he was killed, shot through the eye by a Royalist sniper firing from the top of the Cathedral. The armour that Robert Greville was wearing that day has been preserved here. Also on display are a cavalry helmet said to have belonged to Oliver Cromwell, together with many of the types of armour and weaponry commonly used in the Civil War.

The final section consists of military items from the 1700s and 1800s. Among them are some flintlock 'Brown Bess' muskets with their distinctive triangular socket bayonets. Muskets like these were the standard issue firearm of the British army in the late 18th century, and were given their nickname by the soldiers who carried them.

Although it had been illegal for some time, duelling was still popular among 18th century gentlemen as a means of settling their differences and satisfying their honour. In the latter part of the 1700s, the favoured weapon among duelists was generally the flintlock pistol (there is a pair of duelling pistols on show). Duelling flintlocks differed from other pistols in having an especially light and sensitive trigger, a feature that allowed firing with minimal disturbance to the firing arm and the aim. The collection also includes a superb American Colt pistol, presented to Henry Greville, 3rd Earl of Warwick by Samuel Colt himself, on a visit to the castle in 1851.

All the items and artefacts in the cases are genuine and have been accumulated over hundreds of years by successive Earls of Warwick. Some reproduction pieces have been commissioned so that visitors can handle them or try them on.

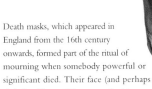

Death masks, which appeared in England from the 16th century onwards, formed part of the ritual of mourning when somebody powerful or significant died. Their face (and perhaps their hands) would be covered with wax then plaster until it dried. The mask would then be used not only as a physical reminder of the person, but also to help symbolise a sense of public commemoration. Oliver Cromwell's mask shows the face of the Lord Protector as it looked just hours after his death in September 1658. It is said that the wood used for the case was salvaged from timbers of the Great Hall roof damaged in the fire of 1871.

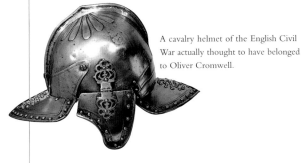

A cavalry helmet of the English Civil War actually thought to have belonged to Oliver Cromwell.

KINGMAKER

ON 2ND MARCH 1450, HENRY VI CONFERRED ON RICHARD NEVILLE, THE HUSBAND OF ANNE DE BEAUCHAMP, THE TITLE EARL OF WARWICK. HISTORY WAS TO KNOW HIM BETTER AS WARWICK THE KINGMAKER.

The Wars of the Roses, which began in the early 1450s and ended with the battle of Bosworth in 1485, were a prolonged struggle for supremacy between the Houses of York and Lancaster.

The conflict had its origins in the increasingly weak rule of the Lancastrian Henry VI. Royal authority slowly evaporated. Into this vacuum at the centre of government poured the political ambitions of several of England's most powerful families. Out of it came civil war, fought to decide who should control the king and, ultimately, who should be king.

Neville's family connections made him a Yorkist. He held a command at the battle of St Albans in 1455 which ended in defeat for the Lancastrians and with the capture of the hapless Henry.

By 1461 the Yorkists had won the first war of succession and Edward, son of the Duke of York, ascended the English throne. As a reward for his help, Warwick rose to a position of great power.

Above: Warwick's letter to Henry Vernon, carrying news of Edward's landing and progress south and summoning him to Coventry with a force of his men-at-arms. The letter is now in a private collection belonging to the Duke of Rutland.

But when Edward IV married Elizabeth Woodville, Warwick found his influence waning. Plotting with Edward's brother, the Duke of Clarence, he raised an army in 1469, took the King prisoner and held him briefly at Warwick Castle.

It proved impossible, however, to rule through a captive Edward who was subsequently released. Warwick fled to France where, deserting his Yorkist allegiances, he offered his services to his old enemy Margaret of Anjou, the exiled wife of Henry VI. He returned to England, put Edward to flight and restored the long imprisoned and much manipulated Henry to the throne.

In March 1471, Edward landed at Ravenspur from the Low Countries with a force of Yorkists and Burgundians to break Warwick's fragile hold on power and reclaim the crown.

On Easter Sunday, 1471, at Barnet, the fortunes of war were to take one final twist for the embattled Kingmaker.

A PREPARATION FOR BATTLE 1471

Richard Neville, Earl of Warwick, was for 16 years a crucial figure in the Wars of the Roses.

In the days before Warwick's army moved south in that Spring of 1471, the castle would have been a hive of activity. Troops had to be summoned and levied. Weapons cleaned and provisions collected.

Like most mediaeval armies, this one was partly made up of the lord's personal guard, usually knights and esquires from the local gentry who were paid a yearly fee for their allegiance in time of war. Each knight brought his own well trained archers and men-at-arms.

Swelling the ranks would be poorer (and often poorly armed) tenants from the estates, liveried yeomen (they weren't paid but fought in return for the Earl's protection) and mercenaries.

Of course, no army however good its soldiers could have marched, let alone fought without its craftsmen and women.

Top: Neville's huge, powerful warhorse, or destrier, is dressed in a caparison bearing the ragged staff emblem of the Earl of Warwick.

Above: Rusted armour, waiting to be polished with leather and powdered pumice to achieve a bright and smooth surface.

Below: The castle's blacksmith plunges a horse shoe, red hot from the forge, into a bucket of water.

Left: In the carpenter's workshop, the wheelwright is planing a new wheel for the cart. "A bad wheelwright makes a good carpenter" went an old saying.

Below: An archer strings his longbow. Edward IV decreed that an archer's bow must be equal to his own height and that archery practice should be compulsory on feast days.

At the heart of the preparations lay the smithy and the armoury. Metal was a precious commodity in the Middle Ages and the men who worked and shaped it enjoyed a high status.

The blacksmith would make sure the warhorses were properly shod while the armourer would make sure the knights were properly protected.

Armour fell into two basic types, mail and plate. Mail consisted of a series of rings skilfully riveted together. A shirt of mail weighed about 13.6 kilograms but it was very flexible, a big advantage when you were fighting hand to hand.

Plate armour was developed later to cope with the advances in longbow technology. Usually it was worn by knights, esquires and the gentry (those, in effect, whose social rank meant they could afford it).

Left: Under the awning of a temporary barn, the cart is being loaded for battle with spacers full of arrows.

Because it was evenly distributed on the wearer, full plate armour didn't actually feel too cumbersome. There was, however, a problem with ventilation (or lack of it) and it was this that sapped the energy when on foot. On horseback, of course, plate was worth its weight for all the protection it offered. Once it had been tempered and shaped, arrows would be fired against the harness (as a suit was called) to test its strength.

Elsewhere, the saws and knives employed in the carpenter's workshop were as vital to an army as the swords and daggers that were honed in the smithy and armoury.

Wheelwrights, for example, would see to it that the baggage carts had good strong wheels needed to make a long journey on the deep rutted tracks that passed for mediaeval roads.

The carpentry workshop was also home to the most destructive weapon of the age: the longbow. Longbows were carved from yew, for its flexibility and strength, and could be as much as six feet in length. Their bow strings were gut or waxed hemp.

Preparing the oak, birch or ash arrows was the job of the fletcher. He would painstakingly attach three goose feathers to the ends of the shafts, either by binding them with fine thread or else sticking them on with bluebell glue.

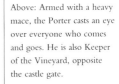

Above: Armed with a heavy mace, the Porter casts an eye over everyone who comes and goes. He is also Keeper of the Vineyard, opposite the castle gate.

Left: An iron breech loading cannon is lowered onto its travelling carriage using a chevre (a mediaeval hoist and pulley).

With the help of horn thimbles, linen thread and brass needles, one seamstress sews a battle standard while another, kneeling, repairs a tent.

A good longbowman would let loose an arrow with metal ripping power. Worse for any advancing cavalry or infantry, he could fire up to 15 every minute.

(By comparison crossbows were slow and complicated, the archer having to use his foot and a winding mechanism to pull the string back and load the 30cm bolt).

It was quite normal for a late mediaeval army to have a large artillery train, though just how effective the field cannons were is another question.

Cannon balls were cut from sandstone using a wooden template or they were moulded from molten iron. Back up ammunition for the gunners consisted of a type of primitive grape shot and huge 1.14m arrows with great iron heads.

For many soldiers, it wasn't only weaponry that mattered on the battlefield. Needlework played its part, too. Retainers would wear a livery or cloth uniform with the badge and colours of their lord sewn on to it. In the confusion of close quarter combat, these liveries were often the only way of telling friend from foe.

Along with most of the castle's clothes and linen, liveries were made, mended and cleaned in an area known as the Wardrobe. Conditions were so filthy everywhere that the better dressed members of the household, like the Keeper of Wardrobe, wore wooden platform shoes or pattens to stop their feet getting covered in mud and dirt.

On the eve of the march, Warwick would probably have eaten with a group of his elite guard of archers. Skilled and disciplined, they ranged in age from teenagers to men with years of campaigning experience behind them.

Left: Standing behind a table, with its counting board and scales, is Warwick's Receiver General, the man usually responsible for collecting rent from the Earl's tenants and now acting as paymaster for the army.

KINGMAKER: THE FINAL ACT

Deserted by the Duke of Clarence a week earlier, Warwick's army, which had been following Edward towards London, reached Barnet during Saturday, 13th April. The Lancastrians numbered some 15,000.

By late evening, the 12,000 strong Yorkist and Burgundian force under Edward had gathered in darkness opposite Warwick's men.

As a watery light filtered across the sky at 4.30am on the morning of Easter Sunday, the facing armies found themselves shrouded in a heavy mist. Fierce fighting began almost immediately.

Initial success, especially on the right, went to the Lancastrians. Confusion and ill-founded suspicions of treachery, however, soon broke out amongst Warwick's ranks. His army fell away and by 8am, with some 3,000 strewn dead on the field, the battle of Barnet was over.

Warwick, caught by Yorkist troops trying to reach his horse, was stripped naked and killed. After two days public viewing in London, he and his brother, Montagu, were buried at Bisham Abbey.

The death of the Kingmaker Earl was mourned by many, but welcomed by more.

Left: A pewter plate, knife, bread and drinking cup, part of the meal Warwick has shared with a group of his elite household archers in a lodging room.

Below: The Earl of Warwick, sword in hand, calls his men to arms for what will be his final battle.

THE TOWERS AND RAMPARTS 🎧 21

THE TOWERS AND CURTAIN WALLS THAT PROTECT THE COURTYARD ARE THE RESULT OF A HUGE RE-STRUCTURING PLAN CARRIED OUT IN THE 14TH AND 15TH CENTURIES.

Built as a fighting platform to repel unwanted visitors, and to protect those within, the mighty towers and ramparts were largely commissioned by the Beauchamp Earls of Warwick who expended vast fortunes on their construction.

Behind the military face, some of the towers also provided sumptuous accommodation for important guests and officials.

BEAR AND CLARENCE TOWERS

Set in the centre of the north wall, these two stunted towers are all that is left of the mighty Tower House which Richard of Gloucester (future King Richard III) started to build in 1478.

It was to have been the same height as Guy's Tower, but twice as wide, with a turret at each of its four corners.

However, this gigantic Royal Keep was intended not just to repel an attack from beyond the walls. It was also designed to protect against a mutinous attack from within the castle itself.

At ground level wells were dug and baking ovens installed, providing the domestic means necessary for those safe inside to endure an attack. In the walls, arrow loops and holes drilled to take cannon are features of the structure's defensive measures.

In 1485 Richard was killed at Bosworth and the building stopped. The Clarence Tower is named after Richard's elder brother, the Duke of Clarence. It is thought that the other tower housed bears that were used for baiting.

Below:
Bear and Clarence Towers.

Left: Caesar's Tower.

RAMPARTS

THE CURTAIN WALLS

The walkways that run along the curtain walls meant that crossbowmen and archers could move swiftly to quell danger at any point on the perimeter.

Once in position they could pick off the enemy from the battlements. These consist of solid sections of wall, called merlons, and gaps, known as embrasures.

The tops of the towers are encircled by parapets that added a further layer to the castle's defences. Cut into the floor of the parapet at regular intervals are openings, or machicolations, through which the garrison could drop stones or pour boiling pitch and quicklime onto the unfortunate attackers below.

On the wall to the right of Clarence Tower is a rare corbelled turret or crow's nest. A watch would be posted there to keep a lookout along the base of the curtain wall.

Left: Machicolations on Caesar's Tower and embrasures, 14th century.

GUY'S TOWER

Towers were the mainstay of a castle's defensive system. Because they projected above and out from the wall, they gave archers a clear view downwards and sideways.

Guy's Tower was built in the 14th century. It is twelve-sided, stands 39m high and has five storeys.

The first four storeys consist of a central stone-vaulted chamber with two small side rooms – one a gardrobe (toilet), the other probably a bedchamber.

The fifth storey is a hexagonal guardroom. During the Civil War the windows here were enlarged so that they could take small hand-held cannons.

THE GATEHOUSE AND BARBICAN 🎧20

Since the entrance to a castle was likely to be a favourite target for an attacking force, it was vital to fortify it as heavily as possible.

The barbican, which had a drawbridge, reaches out into the dry ditch to give the gatehouse more protection.

Soldiers would be faced with the first iron portcullis and a barrage of crossbow bolts. If somehow the barbican portcullis failed to lower, the attackers would find themselves in a narrow roofed passage with arrow slits to either side and, worse, murder holes in the ceiling from which stones and missiles would rain down on them. Colossal wooden doors further prevented them. Those who survived would then have to struggle through raking crossfire up towards the gatehouse itself. Here they would be confronted by yet another portcullis, another set of murder holes and another door.

CAESAR'S TOWER

Built on the orders of Thomas de Beauchamp, Caesar's Tower is a masterpiece of 14th century military architecture.

It has an irregular quatrefoil or cloverleaf shape and rises 44.8m from the solid rock just above the river level. Not including the dungeon, it has three storeys. These are topped by a platform with a crenellated and machicolated parapet.

Behind the parapet there is another storey again which contains a hexagonal guardhouse.

THE DUNGEON 🎧 22

OCCUPYING THE LOWEST CHAMBER OF CAESAR'S TOWER AND BUILT IN THE 14TH CENTURY, IS THE DUNGEON.

Leading from a hatch in the ground at the base of the tower, a single flight of steps provided the way into, and the only way out of, the castle's miserable dungeon.

Beyond a locked door at the foot of the steps, prisoners would endure days, weeks and months, in the small dark space.

A single open drain running across the floor provided the only means of sanitation, whilst the only light to penetrate the gloom came from a tiny shaft high on the wall, and a small window in a chamber, safely behind an iron grill, from where a guard could observe the wretched prisoners.

In a small chamber leading off the main dungeon there is evidence for an even more pitiful existence, reserved for the most deserving of prisoners. The stone-lined pit sunk into the ground may have been an 'oubliette', a lonely and confined space into which a prisoner would be lowered, and left.

Such conditions, however, were not the norm for all prisoners. Senior officers or nobility could expect a reasonable standard of comfort when imprisoned as their confinement would be to grander chambers higher in Caesar's Tower. Such was the protocol of political imprisonment that good treatment of important dignitaries would aid the bargaining process, or ensure similar treatment for yourself should the political tide turn.

Some of the earliest prisoners were reputedly French soldiers from the Hundred Years War, captured for ransom at Poitiers in 1356. Others were Englishmen, Royalists taken during the Civil War. This message is etched into the dungeon wall: *"MasTER johN SMYTH GUNER TO HIS MAJESTYE HighNESS WAS A PRISNER IN THIS PLACE AND LAY HERS froM 1642 TELL th....".*

Above: For a really serious offence a man might be hung alive in chains near the place of the crime until his body entirely rotted away. It is said that many a strong man, who had stood fearless when sentenced to death, broke down completely when measured for his chains.

THE GHOST TOWER 24

FIRST BUILT IN THE 14TH CENTURY TO GUARD AGAINST ENEMY APPROACHES FROM THE RIVER,
THE INTERIOR DECOR REFLECTS THE LATER JACOBEAN STYLE.

A prominent Elizabethan and Jacobean courtier (his poetry, published posthumously
in 1633, won him a reputation also as an important writer), Sir Fulke Greville had
been keen in the early years of his political career to see military action abroad. His
enthusiasm for the venture, however, was repeatedly thwarted by Queen Elizabeth's
insistence that he stay in England.

A late 18th century
portrait of Sir Fulke Greville.

Greville spent a sizeable part of his income (in 1619 it was a colossal £7000 per
year) turning the semi-derelict castle into a stately residence. Work was sufficiently
advanced for James I to be received in 1617 and for Bishop Corbett, a friend who
visited in 1618, to remark of the refurbished castle that "it seems nor art nor force
can intercept it. As if lover built, a soldier kept it".

However generous his spending plans for the castle, it was, tragically, an
accusation of meanness that led to his death in 1628. While in London, an
argument broke out between Greville and one of his servants, Ralph Haywood,
over the contents of Greville's will. Haywood, convinced that his master had not
bequeathed him his rightful due, drew a knife and stabbed Greville. Realising the
enormity of his actions. Haywood fatally turned the blade on himself. After 27
days, Greville also died (despite the efforts of his surgeons).

Greville had once expressed a wish to have tombs built for himself and his friend
and fellow poet, Sir Philip Sidney, in St Paul's Cathedral. In the end it was to the
Church of St Mary in Warwick, that Greville's body was taken and laid to rest in
the tomb he had prepared for himself there. It is said, however, that his ghost still
haunts this tower in which he lodged.

Above: Rich furnishings in
the bed chamber.

Right: Exterior of the
Ghost Tower formerly
known as the
Watergate Tower.

THE STATE ROOMS 🎧40

RETAINING PORTIONS OF THE MEDIAEVAL CASTLE OF THE 14TH CENTURY, THE STATE ROOMS HAVE BEEN EXTENDED, ALTERED AND EMBELLISHED DURING VIRTUALLY EVERY CENTURY SINCE TO LAVISHLY ENTERTAIN THE NOBLEST OF GUESTS, AND TO DISPLAY THE FAMILY'S MOST PRESTIGIOUS POSSESSIONS.

THE CHAPEL 🎧41

SIR FULKE GREVILLE, THE FIRST LORD BROOKE, AUTHORISED THE BUILDING OF THIS SMALL CHAPEL IN THE EARLY 1600S. IT MAY BE ON THE SITE OF ANOTHER CHAPEL FOUNDED AS LONG AGO AS 1119.

This Italian alabaster vase (c.1830) is decorated with classical figures.

Until the turn of this century, the families of the Earls of Warwick would have come here to worship. The servants also used this as their church. Except that they had to stand behind the screen, in the sight of God, but out of the sight of their masters and mistresses.

Behind the altar, the stained glass is mainly mediaeval and was given as a gift by the Earl of Exeter in 1759.

Above the Charles II cupboard is one of the finest examples of wood carving in the castle. It shows the Amazons, a legendary tribe of women warriors, fighting the Greeks. Dated 1740, this Flemish masterpiece was carved by Simon Cognoulles.

The organ was made in Leamington Spa in 1860 by William Downes White. Local skills also went into the pews, altar and the lectern which were carved by Warwick craftsmen.

The colourful decoration of the ceiling only reappeared in 1995 during a restoration programme to correct damp in the Chapel walls. Careful removal of layers of whitewash revealed the series of painted heraldic shields of the Greville family that, according to visitors' journals, were probably installed in the 1740s. When and why they were deliberately hidden we do not know.

One of the stained glass windows, which shows a pickling jar, tells of a legend concerning St Nicholas. Three boys, away studying at a monastery, were journeying home to see their families when the dark skies opened. Seeking shelter from the rain, they stopped at an inn. The innkeeper welcomed them in from the storm but, later, killed the unsuspecting boys and put their bodies in a huge pickling jar. At first light on the next morning, there was a loud knocking at the door. Unfastening the latch, the innkeeper found St Nicholas standing on the threshold. When St Nicholas saw what horrors had been perpetrated, he restored the murdered boys to life.

THE STATE DINING ROOM 🎧42

COMMISSIONED BY FRANCIS GREVILLE IN 1763, THE DINING ROOM WAS DESIGNED AND BUILT BY SOME OF 18TH CENTURY ENGLAND'S FINEST CRAFTSMEN.

Since 1763 this room has seen some impressive dinner parties and some equally distinguished dinner party guests. George IV, for example, dined here, as did Edward VII.

On a visit in 1858, Queen Victoria and Prince Albert had lunch in this room before touring the castle ramparts in the afternoon.

Amongst the six paintings on display, are portraits of Frederick, Prince of Wales (1736) and his wife Augusta, Princess of Saxe-Gotha (1737). Frederick's royal career unfortunately advanced no further than Prince of Wales. The victim of a sporting accident, he was hit by a ball during a game of real tennis and died several months later. Augusta, on the other hand, achieved a more lasting fame. She gave her name to two American cities, one in Georgia and the other in Maine.

At the far end of the room hangs the famous portrait of Charles I on horseback. It is one of five virtually identical pictures produced by Sir Anthony Van Dyck's studio. (If this seems odd, think of it in terms of having more than one print made of a favourite photograph).

The two magnificent lions that hang above the marble Adams fireplace were painted by Frans Snyders. The 18th century cut glass chandelier was made in Murano, Italy. Beneath it, the dining table is English and Victorian.

Portrait of Frederick, Prince of Wales.

During the early 1800s, members of the British nobility would embark on what was known as the Grand Tour, the aim being to broaden the mind.

Right: A detail of the baroque side table covered in gold leaf, made between 1690 and 1710.

Left: A porcelain dish from a 300-piece dessert service, probably purchased in Paris in 1825.

The 'Tour', which usually followed a spectacular scenic route, took in all the great cultural centres of Europe. Henry Greville went on his Tour around 1830. Whilst abroad he bought, along with several large pieces of furniture and some sizeable ornaments, the three marble busts on display here, two of which are Roman Emperors and the other a General.

THE GREAT HALL 🎧43

THE HALL IS THE LARGEST ROOM IN THE CASTLE AND THROUGHOUT
HISTORY HAS BEEN ITS HEART.

It is thought that originally, in the early middle ages, the Great Hall was where
the Cedar Drawing Room is now.

Straw and dirt covered the floor. Burning in the centre of the room would have
been a large fire, its smoke turning the air acrid. The only natural light filtered through
narrow lancet windows. Here it was that the nobility ate, drank and even slept.

The Hall as it stands today, was first constructed in the 14th century. It was
rebuilt in the 17th century and then restored in 1871 after it had been badly
damaged by a fire which swept through part of the castle.

Set against the wall is the magnificent Kenilworth buffet, made in oak by local
craftsmen for the Great Exhibition of 1851. The carved scenes that decorate it,
which include such famous Elizabethans as Philip Sidney, Francis Drake, William
Shakespeare and Walter Raleigh, are reputedly taken from Sir Walter Scott's
19th century historical novel, 'Kenilworth'. After it's display at the Great Exhibition,
where it won the woodcarvers a prize medal for their skill, the buffet was presented
to George, later the 4th Earl of Warwick, in 1852 as a wedding gift from the people
of Warwickshire.

In two of the window bays can be seen superb examples of equestrian armour.
The horse on the left is shown with 16th century Italian armour, and the knight
wears 16th century Italian 'field' (battle) armour. The horse to the right is in a
German 'bard' (armour for a horse) of the 16th century whilst the knight wears
Italian jousting armour circa 1540.

The centre panel of the
Kenilworth Buffet shows
Queen Elizabeth I and her
retinue arriving on a royal visit
to Kenilworth Castle
(8 kilometres from Warwick).

The horse is clad in early 16th century equestrian armour made in Germany. The knight is dressed in heavy Italian jousting armour.

Guy's Porridge Pot.

In the window is a huge cauldron known as 'Guy's Porridge Pot', named after the 10th Earl of Warwick. About 500 years old, it was used to cook stew for the castle's garrison of soldiers.

The miniature suit of armour is said to have been made for the 4-year old son of Robert Dudley, the Earl of Leicester. Also named Robert, he never grew up to fight. He died at the age of 6 from one of the many illnesses that made war on children and from which there was no protection.

Made for the child of a wealthy courtier, this exquisite ceremonial harness was probably commissioned from the Greenwich workshops, the premier manufactory of armour for England's Royalty and high nobility. Tradition tells that it belonged to Robert Dudley affectionately known as the 'Noble Impe' the infant son of Robert Dudley, Earl of Leicester, court favourite of Queen Elizabeth I.

Left: German 'Maxmilian' armour, c.1520.

THE RED DRAWING ROOM 🎧44

WITH ITS RED LACQUER PANELLING, THIS IS THE FIRST OF THE FIVE STATE ROOMS
WHICH ROBERT GREVILLE REFURBISHED IN THE LATE 17TH CENTURY.

To the left of the fireplace hangs a portrait of Ambrosio Spinola, from the school
of Rubens. Born in Italy, Spinola (1569-1630) made his name as a soldier serving
with the Spanish armies in Flanders.

On the adjacent wall you can see a picture of Sir Philip Sidney (1554-1586).
A renowned poet and soldier, and a close friend of Sir Fulke Greville, he was
regarded as almost the perfect Elizabethan courtier.

The main painting in the room is of Jeanne d'Aragon, granddaughter of King
Ferdinand IV of Naples. Feted as one of the most beautiful women in 16th century
Europe, she was also clever, witty and powerful.

Either side of the fireplace are two Italian chests called 'cassoni'. Fitted to the
front of these chests are painted panels that are much earlier than the chests
themselves. Painted in Italy in the late 15th century they were probably removed
from a religious building and are the oldest paintings in the castle collection.

Hanging above the
marble Adams fireplace is
a beautiful Louis XV
bracket clock decorated
with Boulle marquetry.

Above: Although a
Scottish Covenanter,
James Graham, Marquis
of Montrose (painted by
William Dobson), stayed
loyal to Charles I during
the English Civil War.
After 5 years of exile
he returned home to
his execution in 1650.
His armour is now in
the Great Hall.

THE CEDAR DRAWING ROOM 🎧45

THE INTRICATE CEDAR PANELLING, WHICH GIVES THE ROOM ITS NAME, WAS COMPLETED SOME TIME IN THE 1670S BY TWO LOCAL MEN, WILLIAM AND ROGER HURLBULT.

Although it is Italian in style, the magnificently elaborate plaster ceiling was actually executed by English craftsmen over 300 years ago.

If you look down at the floor, you will see a fabulous example of 19th century French carpet making. It was woven in one piece at Aubusson. Worked into each corner is the Bear and Ragged Staff emblem of the Earls of Warwick, while running along the sides is the Swan crest of the Greville family.

The two side tables beneath the paintings are both Chippendale, as are four of the eight sets of wall lights.

One of the bronze heads is of Elfrida who later became Countess of Warwick. Elfrida was the sister of Sir Anthony Eden, British Prime Minister in the 1950s.

With a single exception, all the delicately fashioned 18th century chandeliers are English. The one in the centre is Irish crystal from Waterford.

Portrait of King Charles I whose defeat in the English Civil War led to his execution in 1649.

Dating from the 17th century, the legs of this Florentine table show a pregnant woman. Her condition becomes increasingly obvious with each leg.

Above: The beautifully decorated Japanese Imari banqueting bowls were made in Arita in about 1690.

THE GREEN DRAWING ROOM 🎧46

SO CALLED BECAUSE OF ITS GREEN PAINTED PANELLING, THE ROOM'S 18TH CENTURY CEILING IS 'COFFERED' OR MADE UP OF OCTAGONAL SUNKEN PANELS, EACH WITH ITS OWN CENTRAL MOTIF.

In the centre stands a superb Italian table. It was made in Florence sometime in the 1500s and the top is beautifully inlaid with exotic semi-precious stones such as jasper, agate and lapis lazuli.

The main story the Green Drawing Room has to tell does not lie in its furniture, though. It is told through its paintings. As you scan the walls, what you see is a brief snapshot of that profoundly traumatic event, the English Civil War.

At the outbreak of hostilities, Warwick Castle was owned by Robert Greville, Baron Brooke. A Parliamentarian, he was killed by a sniper's bullet at Lichfield in 1643. The oval paintings over the door are of his three sons. On the bottom row is Sir Peter Lely's portrait of Prince Rupert of the Rhine, Charles I's nephew and one of his top generals.

Either side of the fireplace are pictures of King Charles I and his wife, Henrietta Maria. Like many of the paintings in the room, they are from the school of Van Dyck.

Of course, most of the men and women who perished in the conflict left few, if any, records of their lives. These pictures are a reminder to us of a whole generation.

The 18th century 'coffered' ceiling which is thought to have been inspired by the Roman ruins at Palmyra in Syria.

The quality of these tapestries is evident in the degree of detail, and the vibrancy of the colours. An unusual feature of the tapestry is the method employed for fixing the natural dyes required for the colours. In order to prevent the colours from running urine was added, this being the best treatment available at the time. A man was even paid to drink large quantities of beer so that an adequate supply was available.

THE QUEEN ANNE BEDROOM 🎧47
IT ACTUALLY TAKES ITS NAME NOT FROM QUEEN ANNE HERSELF, BUT FROM HER BED.

According to tradition Queen Anne was to have visited Warwick Castle in 1704 and, by way of preparation, her state bed was sent on in advance from Windsor. Although the planned visit was cancelled, the magnificent royal bed stayed on. In 1773 King George III made a permanent gift of it to Francis, the then Earl of Warwick.

The bed hangings are of crimson velvet with sea-green panels. Standing near the bed is one of the Queen's leather-covered travelling chests.

Sadly, Queen Anne's life wasn't the happiest. Of her 17 children, all save one died in infancy.

The contrast between the cathedral-like bed and the child-size pieces of furniture could not be more striking. They may look like toys, but, in fact, they are samples used by 18th century travelling salesmen.

Decorating the walls are some of the most interesting treasures in the entire castle: Delft tapestries, dating from 1604, depicting palace gardens.

Queen Anne's travelling chest displaying her initials.

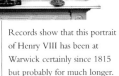

THE BLUE BOUDOIR 🎧48

THE LAST OF THE STATE ROOMS, THE BLUE BOUDOIR TODAY LOOKS MUCH AS IT DID IN THE 1870S.

Dominating this room is an important picture of King Henry VIII, from the studio of Hans Holbein, which is painted on wooden panels and shows the king in his early forties.

The swags of fruit and foliage that surround the picture were the work of Warwick woodcarvers. Fine examples of work produced by the many woodcarving firms that once operated in Warwick can be found in several parts of the castle. Opposite the fireplace, however, the carved decorations on the wall are traditionally said to be by Grinling Gibbons (1648-1721), the celebrated carver with numerous Royal commissions to his name.

To the left of the king are two portraits of the Boleyn sisters, Mary and Anne, both dating from the 18th century. Mary was certainly his mistress and might well have had an illegitimate son by him. Anne was the younger sister and became Henry's second, ill-fated wife in 1533. She bore him a daughter, the future Queen Elizabeth I. Three years later, she was beheaded on the king's orders.

Records show that this portrait of Henry VIII has been at Warwick certainly since 1815 but probably for much longer.

This beautiful silver faced clock is said to have belonged to Marie Antoinette who, in 1793, went to the guillotine with her husband Louis XVI in revolutionary France. Two hundred years on, it still keeps good time.

A ROYAL WEEKEND PARTY, 1898

IN THE 1890S, UNDER THE GUIDING (AND LAVISH) HAND OF FRANCES, FONDLY KNOWN AS 'DAISY', COUNTESS OF WARWICK, THE CASTLE BECAME A FAVOURITE RETREAT FOR SOME OF THE MOST IMPORTANT FIGURES IN LATE VICTORIAN SOCIETY.

In 1898, the countess hosted a weekend party at which the principal guest was the Prince of Wales, later Edward VII. In the next twelve rooms, or former private apartments, you will see a re-creation of that weekend. Most of the furnishings and the fittings are those that were actually here in 1898. Photographs and inventories from the period have helped recreate the layouts of the rooms as you see today.

THE LIBRARY

It is early afternoon and the gentlemen have been discussing politics. Daisy, Countess of Warwick, has breached etiquette by riding in the morning and missing lunch. She has just entered the library to apologise and to make arrangements for the coming evening.

   At the far end of the room, a young Winston Churchill scans a book. Only 23, he did not enter Parliament until 1900. Forty years and a lifetime later, he became Prime Minister during the Second World War.

   Spencer Cavendish, the Duke of Devonshire, owner of Chatsworth House, is the only man seated. Cavendish was an influential Liberal Member of Parliament and during the 1880s held office, first as Secretary for India and then as Secretary for War. The 16-year-old figure is of Leopold Lord Brooke, (known as Guy) Francis Greville's eldest son. He left Eton the following year to join the British Army in Africa during the second Boer war. He became Earl of Warwick in 1924 only to die four years later, his life wrecked by alcoholism.

A photograph of a weekend party taken in 1897. The Countess of Warwick is seated fourth from the left. Edward, Prince of Wales, stands sixth from the left.

THE MUSIC ROOM

In the music room, other guests are listening to Clara Butt, one of the most famous singers of her day who stood at 1.88m in her stockinged feet. She is accompanied on the piano by Paolo Tosti, music master to the Royal family.

   The young girl turning the pages is Lady Marjorie Greville, the eldest daughter of the Earl and Countess of Warwick.

   On the sofa, sitting next to the Duchess of Devonshire, is Lady Randolph Churchill. Born Jennie Jerome, an American, Lady Churchill was Winston's mother and was widowed in 1895.

   George Cornwallis-West, an officer in the Scots Guards and heir to Ruthin Castle, stands behind the two ladies. Roughly the same age as her son, Cornwallis-West later married Jennie Churchill.

THE SMOKING ROOM

Charles Spencer Churchill, the 9th Duke of Marlborough and owner of Blenheim Palace, was Under-Secretary for the Colonies between 1903 and 1905. Across the room from him sits his opponent at cards, the Duke of York. George was the second son of Edward VII, then still the Prince of Wales. He reigned as George V from 1910 to 1936.

THE LADIES' BOUDOIR

In the more feminine surroundings of the Boudoir, Daisy's half sister Millicent, Duchess of Sutherland takes tea, while Lady Sackville-West catches up with her correspondence.

Millicent was married on her 17th birthday and went to France four days after the declaration of World War One to work for the Red Cross.

Victoria, Lady Sackville-West, was the daughter of an aristocratic diplomat and a Spanish dancer. Despite being married, Victoria was linked with some of the most illustrious men of the day.

The room reflects Daisy's passion for all things French. The suite of furniture is French; the panelling and fireplace were imported from a French chateau.

Daisy soon established herself as a star on the social scene, especially with the Marlborough House set, a group gathered around Edward, Prince of Wales. Rumour even had it that Edward and Daisy were lovers.

In February 1895, the Countess organised a spectacular costume ball at Warwick Castle to which all 400 guests came dressed as 18th century French courtiers. That winter had been especially hard and in the town unemployment was high and hunger widespread. The ball drew an avalanche of criticism and it marked the start of her conversion to the Labour party. Original photographs of many of the guests at this party, resplendent in their expensive costumes, can be seen upstairs on the final landing.

Over the years Daisy became a vegetarian, championed women's education and stood as a Labour candidate.

Portrait of Daisy, Countess of Warwick.

DAISY'S BEDROOM

Upstairs the hosts and guests alike are preparing for dinner in the State Dining Room. The weekend party is an important social occasion, and for it Daisy has decided on a new gown she has commissioned from Jean Worth, one of the top European couturiers of the day. Daisy's bedroom mirrors her love of the fashions of the day. Nowhere to be seen are the dark, heavy reds and greens of high Victorian décor. The room instead is graced with the lighter, fresher colours and fabrics that represent the 1890s design at its most modish.

THE CARNATION BEDROOM

In the Carnation Bedroom, Field Marshall Lord Roberts is also readying himself for the evening. Roberts was born in Cawnpore. After an education at Eton, he returned to India to serve in the army and saw action during the Indian Mutiny (1857) for which he was twice decorated with the Victoria Cross. He went on to become one of the best known of a cohort of famous Victorian generals, and ended a distinguished military career as Commander-in-Chief of the British Army. Here he is seen wearing the order of St Patrick, an honour he received in 1897.

A working day for a Victorian housemaid would begin at between five and six in the morning. During a busy weekend, such as this, the housemaid would be expected to carry out various duties from opening shutters and windows, to searching the beds for unwelcome insects. When there was company, the maid was expected to help in any way that the housekeeper instructed. Taking a quick glance out of the window, although against the rules, would perhaps be the only chance in a busy day for the maid to witness the aristocracy at leisure.

THE DOWAGER'S BEDROOM 🎧 36

A lamp shines on the dressing table of Anne, the Dowager Countess, while a maid dresses her hair in plaits. The widow of George Greville, the 4th Earl of Warwick, the countess no longer lived at the castle, having chosen to move to her London residence in 1893. Daisy, however, kept this bedroom for Anne whenever she visited. Perhaps the most striking feature of the room, is the number of paintings on the walls, testifying to the countess' enjoyment of art. A talented artist, Anne had several of her own works exhibited at the Royal Academy, and her portrait of her son, Sidney, now hangs in the Smoking Room.

THE EARL'S DRESSING ROOM 🎧 37

In the Earl's dressing room, Francis Greville, cigar in hand, is waiting for his bath to be drawn. He married Daisy in 1881 and became Earl of Warwick in 1893. As Lord Brooke, he spent part of his career in politics, representing first East Somerset and then Colchester as a Conservative MP before leaving Parliament in 1892.

More enthusiastic than astute as a businessman, he invested in several ventures and managed to lose a small fortune in the process. He was dogged by constant ill-health, and lived his last years as an invalid.

THE KENILWORTH BEDROOM

Edward, the Prince of Wales, was such a frequent visitor to Warwick Castle
that a bedroom was specially set aside for him. Named after Kenilworth Castle
from where portions of the Tudor panelling came, it's rich furnishings and
grand stone hearth make this a suitably imposing room.

The eldest son of Queen Victoria, Edward was crowned King in 1901
and ruled until his death in 1910. Before going down to dinner he discusses
matters of the day with Lord Curzon who was made Viceroy of India in 1898
and later served as Foreign Secretary.

THE CHINESE BEDROOM

Saying goodnight to her baby son in the Chinese bedroom is Consuelo, Duchess
of Marlborough and firm friend of the Countess of Warwick. A daughter of
the wealthy Vanderbilts of New York, Consuelo married Charles Spencer-
Churchill in 1895.

The bedroom is generously adorned with oriental motifs and references.
The screen and the painted panel over the hearth show traditional Far Eastern
scenes. Chinese ornaments sit on shelves and fill niches, while the canopy covering
the four poster bed is extravagantly topped with a pagoda-inspired tower.

MILL & ENGINE HOUSE

THE WARWICK CASTLE MILL AND ENGINE HOUSE OPENED TO THE PUBLIC FOR THE FIRST TIME IN APRIL 2002. THE EARLIEST RECORDED MILL AT THE CASTLE, DATES FROM THE EARLY 12TH CENTURY.

The Warwick Castle Mill and Engine House opened to the public for the first time in April following a lengthy and costly programme of restoration.

The earliest known Mill at the Castle, recorded in the early 12th century, was approximately 100 yards downstream of the Castle buildings. By the late 14th century this position was abandoned in favour of the present site.

In the second half of the 18th century the site underwent an architectural transformation as the half-timbered structure was replaced in favour of the more fashionable Gothic building seen today, its style mirroring the Castle's towers and ramparts above.

The Mill remained largely unchanged until a fire in 1880 that destroyed all internal milling machinery, leaving nothing but the waterwheel and outer walls standing. Despite this tragedy, fourteen years later the latest technology made use of the Mill's space and its riverside location, in the form of a water-powered electric generating plant, one of the earliest hydroelectric power stations in the country.

The Mill and Engine House reveals a little-known chapter of the Castle's history and shows how the innovative and extravagant Earl of Warwick was able to generate electricity for the Castle, including the lighting of the whole Castle for his wife's birthday.

The Castle continued to depend on the Mill and Engine House for its electrical power until the arrival of mains electricity in 1940 which signalled the gradual demise of the plant, leading to complete abandonment in 1954.

Now, at a cost of over £2million, the Mill and Engine House project has returned the historic building and machines to their former glory. Recreating the electrical powerplant of the Castle's Victorian age was a challenge. For example, only one firm in the country possessed the necessary expertise and equipment to produce the hand-rolled, wrought iron blades required for the restoration of the waterwheel. The Crossley Gas Engines are so keenly sought-after by collectors from the USA, that sourcing originals for the Engine House was even more difficult.

Despite such obstacles, with time and energy, scores of professionals over the years have succeeded in restoring our heritage for future generations, using revenue from visitor admissions to conserve this unique example of Victorian innovation.

Left: There is an ancient connection between mills and eels and this mill is no exception – it has its own trap and the eels caught were served to the guests of the Earl and Countess.

Below: Crossley Gas Engines in the Mill & Engine House.

THE GROUNDS 🎧26

IN THE 1750S THE 1ST EARL OF WARWICK AND LANCELOT 'CAPABILITY' BROWN CREATED THE
LANDSCAPE GROUNDS. TO THIS DAY, THE FRUITS OF THEIR LABOURS ARE CLEARLY EVIDENT.

For the first 400 years of its existence, Warwick Castle had an overriding purpose, to keep those on the inside safe from those on the outside. It was a centre of military power in a land where warfare was a way of conducting political, religious and even personal affairs. Everything, therefore, was geared towards making the castle an impregnable fortress. And that, literally, meant no place for a garden as we understand it.

But as the temper of the times softened, so people's attitudes towards their domestic environment changed. Warwick Castle came to be seen as less of a fortress and more of a home. The first mention of a garden comes in a survey of 1576. It talks of the "queen's gardens next Avon without the castle wall," which suggest they lay somewhere between the Mound and the river. The likelihood is that they were specially prepared for the visit, in August 1572, of Elizabeth I, and would have consisted of a series of coloured gravel pathways, leading between very formal patterns, or knots, of herbs and shrubs.

From 1604 to 1628, Fulke Greville's renovation of the castle saw the planting of new gardens that, according to a contemporary account, were without parallel in this part of England. During the Civil War, these were dug up for gun emplacements by the garrison defending the castle. Only as the castle transformed from a fortress to a stately home, did Warwick Castle's grounds and gardens blossom. The transformation was down to one of Britain's greatest landscape gardeners, Lancelot 'Capability' Brown.

It is believed that Warwick Castle was Brown's first independent castle commission and his achievements here during the 1750s won him praise and national recognition. Brown's genius lay in the way he turned the grounds into an imaginative extension of the grandeur and the scale of the castle.

It may look natural, but the curved sweep of the lawns down from the castle to the river is man-made. Specially chosen trees and shrubs were planted to create a frame for the castle and the landscape. The courtyard was also raised by several feet to give it a more classically balanced look.

Although there have been many changes since Brown's time, the overall layout, with its vistas, mounds and copses, is his, a living work of art.

THE MOUND

First built in 1068 on the orders of William the Conqueror, it formed the most important part of the Norman castle's defence system.

Advances in military architecture, however, made it more and more of an outpost. By the 17th century, it had been absorbed within Sir Fulke Greville's garden, topped by a single Scots pine.

Today, it is the perfect vantage point, not for defending against marauding English troops, but for taking in the beautiful unfolding views of these peaceful grounds.

THE CONSERVATORY

The beautifully proportioned conservatory, which acts as a focal point in the landscape, was built in 1786 by a local mason, William Eborall.

Originally, it was designed as a home for the Warwick Vase, a magnificent piece of ancient Roman pottery excavated near Tivoli in 1771.

The original vase is now on display at the Burrell Collection in Glasgow. There is, however, a full-size replica standing in the conservatory, which has since been converted back to its Victorian use as an ornamental glasshouse for growing exotic plants.

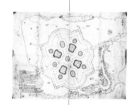

THE VICTORIAN ROSE GARDEN

First laid down in 1868, the Rose Garden, like the Peacock Garden was designed by Robert Marnock.

By the end of the Second World War, though, it had disappeared under a tennis court. Fortunately, two of Marnock's original drawings survived, so the plot was lovingly brought back to life in 1986. Its charm stems from the contrast between the very precise geometry and proportions of the beds and the garden's informal, almost secretive setting.

The roses are all of the old-fashioned type, many of them popular with the Victorians. To commemorate the recreation of the garden, 120 years on, a new English rose was bred and named 'Warwick Castle'. The best time to see the display is in late June and the whole of July.

The pair of unusual icehouses date back to 1830s and were built in the earth bank facing away from the sun. They were still being used in 1869 when in December of that year 16s 4d allowance was paid 'to men filling the ice houses'.

Copy of original plans by Robert Marnock for the Victorian Rose Garden.

Aerial view of Warwick Castle and Victorian Rose Garden.

Left: Victorian Rose Garden in full bloom.

THE PEACOCK GARDEN AND PAGEANT FIELD

Directly in front of the conservatory is the Peacock Garden, designed by the Victorian landscape gardener Robert Marnock.

Just to the south-east is a group of trees that includes a Wellingtonia planted by Prince Albert in 1858. Queen Victoria also planted an oak which stands close to the driveway from the courtyard. Just 18.3m from this magnificent oak is a young oak tree which was planted on 1 January 2000 to celebrate the coming of a new century.

Running gently down to the river is the Pageant Field, flanked on either side by trees, of which some, like the Cedars of Lebanon, are over 200 years old.

RIVER AND ISLAND

Downstream from the mill, a bridge takes you across the Avon and onto the island.

In the 1890s, the island used to be inhabited by, amongst others, some Japanese deer, a flock of Chinese geese, an emu, assorted raccoons, an ant bear and a baby elephant.

They were part of a menagerie collected by the Countess of Warwick. The elephant got rather big, as elephants do, and had to be given to an animal trainer in Leamington. The emu, on the other hand, entered the pages of emu history by chasing a bishop through the castle grounds.

The popular activity of pleasure boating saw much innovation at Warwick Castle when the Earl and Countess purchased an electric launch. Delivered to the castle by the Great Western Railway company in 1898, the luxurious launch had comfortable fittings, such as carpets, blinds and awnings and was powered by a number of batteries which were re-charged in the millhouse.

WARWICK CASTLE TODAY

WARWICK CASTLE WAS BOUGHT BY THE TUSSAUDS GROUP IN NOVEMBER 1978. THE 36TH EARL OF WARWICK, CHARLES GUY GREVILLE AND HIS FAMILY LIVED IN THE CASTLE AT THE TIME AND IT WAS HIS SON, DAVID GREVILLE WHO SOLD THE CASTLE.

Since 1978, The Tussauds Group has developed the castle into one of the top UK tourist attractions receiving around 800,000 guests each year. The castle is a Scheduled Ancient Monument and Grade 1 listed building and The Tussauds Group ensures that the castle is maintained on an ongoing basis as an outstanding centuries-old monument for future generations to enjoy. Maintaining a national monument involves extensive costs and the castle receives no grants or financial support from the government or any public body. Over £20m has been spent on repairs, restoration and refurbishment since The Tussauds Group acquired the castle and funds for this work are raised solely from guests admission revenue.

Special events and entertainment have been taking place in the castle grounds since the early 1970s. Today the programme of events has been extended to include a variety of entertainment throughout the year. This includes mediaeval Jousting Tournaments, Birds of Prey displays and a variety of castle characters.

Over the centuries Warwick Castle has hosted many lavish events and high society dinners. In 1996 there was a special lunch in the State Dining Room for HM Queen Elizabeth II and HRH The Duke of Edinburgh during a visit to the castle. Today we welcome evening guests for a variety of events organised by both businesses and individuals who wish to celebrate in style. From the 14th century Great Hall for that unique dinner for 130 guests, to the more elegant dining in the State Dining Room for 30 guests. Also the popular themed evenings – Mediaeval, 'Kingmaker's feast' and our Georgian, 'Highwayman's Supper' are held in the Undercroft and Coach House respectively.

Each year on the Pageant Field we host a 'Grand Summer Concert and Fireworks Display' – an evening of classical music with a fireworks finale held in conjunction with the Warwick and Leamington Festival.